The Goddess Guide to
Chakra Vitality

The Goddess Guide to Chakra Vitality
3rd edition © Anita Revel

ISBN 978-0-578-02666-4

First published © Anita Ryan 2003
Second edition © Anita Ryan-Revel 2006
Third edition © Anita Revel 2009

Published by	Now Age Publishing Pty Ltd
	NowAgePublishing.com
Edited by	Shamana Love
Cover by	Inspired Insight
	inspired-insight.com
Cover illustration by	Anita Revel
	AnitaRevel.com
Yoga illustrations by	Lisa M Brennan (LMB & Co.)
Contact the publisher at	PO Box 1800
	Margaret River 6285
	Western Australia

The Goddess Guide to
Chakra Vitality

ANITA REVEL

Books by the same author

Moon Goddess, Manifest Your Dreams
(Goddess.com.au   August 2006)

Selena's Crystal Balls,
A Magical Journey Through the Chakras
(Goddess.com.au   March 2007)

Outing the Goddess Within,
One Girl's Journey With 52 Guides
(Goddess.com.au   January 2008)

The 7-Day Chakra Workout
(ChakraGoddess.com April 2008)

Sacred Vigilance, Wide-Awake Meditation
(Goddess.com.au   September 2008)

Goddess At Play, A Journal For Self-Discovery and Play
(Goddess.com.au   February 2009)

What Would Goddess Do?
A Journal for Channelling Divine Guidance
(Goddess.com.au   March 2009)

The Goddess DIET
See a Goddess in the Mirror in 21 Days
(Now Age Publishing June 2009)

The Goddess Guide to
Chakra Vitality

Through honouring the Feminine Divine, we reconnect with our inner goddess. We respect and empower ourselves spiritually, psychologically, emotionally, and physically.

Keeping our chakras healthy and energised is one way to nurture the inner goddess and achieve balance in our work, home and social lives.

In this book you can expect to learn about the seven essential aspects of life; how to promote a state of harmony and peace of mind by bringing the chakras into balance; how goddess energy empowers you to master these major aspects; how to recognise which ancient goddess role model is impacting your choices and habits; and how to incorporate this goddess energy into daily life and situations.

The Goddess Guide to Chakra Vitality has been developed to equip you with the basics of chakra health so that you can shine with a goddess glow day in, day out.

Love and blissings,

Anita Revel.

This book is dedicated to you and
your inner goddess... She of a
thousand colours, limitless hues,
tasty tones and shades of bliss.
She of ragged starbursts,
spontaneous snoozes, guerilla acts
of altruism, and wild yearnings
for mother earth love.

I intend for you uninhibited
happiness, good health and giggles,
sufficient warmth, and an
unbreakable connection with the
mother matrix. May you radiate
your light for happily ever after.

Love and blissings,

Anita xx

Offerings

What is a Chakra?

When you see the colour red, do you think "Danger danger Will Robinson", or do you think about love, passion and all the good stuff in between?

Either response would be appropriate. Red is a power colour that is related to the base chakra – the energy centre that gives us a sense of grounding, of security, of loving our path in life, and of course, passion.

The base chakra is one of seven major chakras, and yes, everyone has them. They are spinning wheels of light and energy that respond to colour, essential oils, musical tones, gemstones, mantras, body movements and more. When the seven chakras are all vibrating at their ideal level, you are able to feel a deep-seated contentedness, even bliss.

The seven major chakras and their domains are as follows:

Base	Self-preservation
Sacral	Self-gratification
Solar Plexus	Self-definition
Heart	Self-acceptance
Throat	Self-expression
Third Eye	Self-reflection
Crown	Self-knowledge

When all chakras are balanced and spinning at their optimum vibration level, they integrate physical, emotional, psychological and spiritual facets of the human into a coherent whole.

There is generally an overlapping and sharing of functions amongst chakras, both physiologically and psychologically.

Location of Each Chakra

The chakras are located roughly near our glands along the meridian of our body. The name of each chakra describes roughly where it is located.

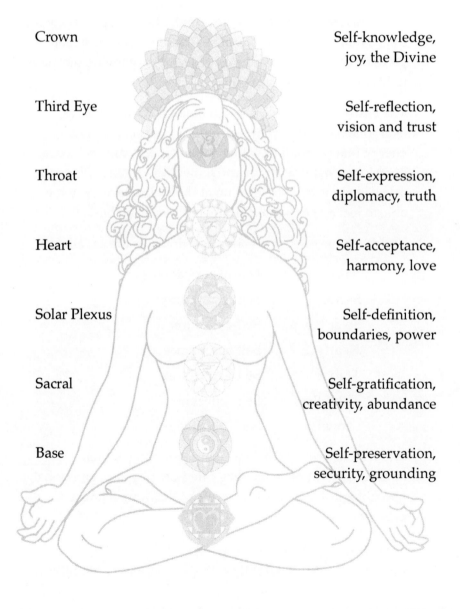

Crown	Self-knowledge, joy, the Divine
Third Eye	Self-reflection, vision and trust
Throat	Self-expression, diplomacy, truth
Heart	Self-acceptance, harmony, love
Solar Plexus	Self-definition, boundaries, power
Sacral	Self-gratification, creativity, abundance
Base	Self-preservation, security, grounding

Physiological Role of Each Chakra

The base and sacral chakras are related to generative and sexual functions, while the solar plexus chakra is related to the stomach and digestion.

The heart chakra is related to the heart and circulation, and the throat chakra is related to the lungs and the voice, including the ears, nose, throat and thyroid glands.

The third eye chakra is related to vision, the eyes, and the pituitary gland, while the crown chakra is related to the brain, and especially the pituitary and pineal glands.

Psychological Role of Each Chakra

The three lower chakras are related to our raw emotions and biological instincts ranging from sexual desire and hunger, into passion, anger, pleasure and joy and other relatively simple emotional states.

The four higher chakras are related to higher cognitive states. That is, the heart chakra is related to empathy and understanding; the throat chakra is related to vocal expression, hearing, and the ability to communicate; the third eye chakra is related to clarity and the ability to understand; and the crown chakra is related to deep understanding and comprehension on a spiritual level.

I also like to think of the chakras as rulers of the seven essential aspects of life: security, creativity, power, love, truth, trust and joy. If I become aware that a chakra is out of balance, I immediately associate it with the relevant life aspect to identify issues that need resolving or healing. For example, if my solar plexus chakra were out of balance, I'd look for signs of manipulation, disrespect, causes of anxiety, or events that disconnect me from my authentic self.

Characteristics of Each Chakra

Base

Located at the base of the spine, this chakra forms our foundation. Related to our survival instincts, it represents our sense of grounding and connection to our bodies and the physical plane.

Ideally this chakra brings us health, prosperity, security, and a sense of belonging – to family, to the community, to humanity, and to Gaia and her living creatures.

Typically this chakra can go out of balance when you are in situations that threaten your security – for example, changing jobs, moving home, or losing a loved one who you depended on. If you ever feel unsettled, or that you are at a crossroads, raise your conscious focus on your base chakra.

Sacral

The second chakra, located in the abdomen, lower back, and sexual organs, is related to creativity, emotions, abundance and sexuality.

This chakra brings us fluidity and grace, depth of feeling, sexual fulfilment, and the ability to accept change. It connects us to others through feeling, desire, sensation, and movement.

Linked to the reproductive area of the female body, creativity is heightened when this chakra is awakened. It also promotes an appreciation of the wondrous feminine divine. It can therefore go out of balance if you are the type to look in the mirror and only see 'imperfections', or if you believe yourself to be less of a person simply because you're not 'beautiful' enough to grace a magazine cover.

Solar Plexus

This chakra is known as the power chakra. It rules our personal power, will, fear, autonomy and metabolism.

When vibrating at its optimum level, this chakra brings us energy, effectiveness, spontaneity, and non-dominating power. This may also be described as a healthy sense of self.

Personal power is physically noticeable in the solar plexus chakra – the place where anxiety manifests as a nervous energy also known as butterflies.

If you're feeling manipulated or ignored, this threatens your self-definition – this in turn results in anxiety and reduced vitality.

But when the solar plexus chakra is charged, it is easy to feel invincible as the life of the party.

Heart

This chakra is related to love and is the integrator of opposites in the psyche: mind and body, male and female, persona and shadow, ego and unity, giving and receiving.

A healthy fourth chakra produces enhanced empathetic abilities. It also allows us to love deeply, feel compassion and enjoy a deep sense of peace and harmony.

Trust issues, betrayals, rejections, self-criticism or perceived wrongs will put your heart chakra out of balance. If you find it difficult to connect with others in a meaningful way, think about ways to energise your heart chakra to promote more honest connections. Above all, learn to accept and love yourself unconditionally in order to attract the deep love you deserve from others.

Throat

The throat chakra is related to communication, courage and creative connection.

A healthy throat chakra facilitates diplomatic and graceful expression. It gives you the courage to say what needs to be said without the fear of consequence.

The throat chakra also leads to clairaudience, which is the ability to hear on the non-physical planes. Ignoring the 'voices' of Angels and other spiritual beings will also serve to block your throat chakra.

Trust and honour higher forces at work within you to keep your throat chakra open and vibrant.

Third Eye

This chakra is related to the act of seeing, both physically and intuitively. As such it opens our psychic faculties and our understanding of archetypal levels.

The awakening of the third-eye chakra leads to clairvoyance or the ability to see on the non-physical planes.

When vibrant and alert it allows us to experience clarity, in effect, letting us 'see the big picture' and understand your place in the world. It also assists in studies, negotiations and communication of truth.

Any self-doubt is a guaranteed way to block the third-eye chakra. First and foremost, you must accept that your intuition, your inherent wisdom, has led you to make the right decisions. By going against your instincts, you effectively shut down your third eye chakra.

Crown

There are many forms of knowledge – cognitive, emotional, intuitive, learned, to name a few. But 'wisdom' is a whole new level of understanding that transcends the physical plane.

This is the crown chakra that relates to consciousness as pure awareness. It is our connection to the greater world beyond, to a timeless, spaceless place of all-knowing.

When awakened, this chakra brings us knowledge, wisdom, understanding, spiritual connection, and bliss.

An open crown chakra is also associated with the ability to consciously travel on the non-physical planes (astral travel).

Learn More

To learn more about the major chakras and how their status influences everyday life, register for the free online e-Course, The 7-Day Chakra Workout, at ChakraGoddess.com

This is a revolutionary e-Course that prompts you to master the seven essential aspects of life that are anchored in the chakra realms. Learn more about the seven essential tools to activate and balance your chakras, ideas for how to use these tools, and how to bring it all together so that all aspects of your life are aligned in harmony.

I developed this Chakra Workout by adapting ancient theories and applying them to modern practice. The tips, tools and exercises in the full version of the Workout are based on my personal experience and journey that led me where I am today – happy, healthy and in harmony with the seven essential aspects of life. Enjoy :-)

Domains of Each Chakra

The ancient goddesses were honoured for many reasons – for an abundant harvest, to keep the family and home safe, or to escort souls safely to the after-life to name a few. In this modern age, however, it isn't always practical to pray at a moonlit forest temple or to burn bonfires during an outdoor springtime orgy.

So how else can a modern gal reconnect with the ancient goddess energy and manifest in her modern life?

Simple. By being aware of yourself and making choices with intention. Every action, thought, projection of self, and treatment of others is a reflection of the goddess within.

Being 'goddess' is about channelling and showing the strengths of the real You. Aim to raise your consciousness of goddess energy to radiate confidence, innate beauty and inspired joy – your authentic self.

There are seven aspects of *self* that should be considered to fulfil a balanced and enriching existence. Follow these tips to live each day as a modern goddess.

Self Preservation

Being goddess is about being in tune with oneself, being able to recognise threatening situations and respond rationally and calmly. Be conscious of the influence of others' moods and needs and stay balanced in times of duress. Trust your instinct and act with the confidence that comes from a deep-seated connection with earth. Manifest a dynamic presence by walking confidently on your path, and feel secure by keeping your feet firmly on the ground. Get into the habit of consciously coming back to 'centre' in any unsettling situations – use the mantra 'Centre' if it suits.

Self Gratification

Creatively, emotionally and sexually, connect with others through feeling, desire, sensation and movement. Learn to accept change gracefully, release anxieties and past hurts, and don't be afraid to let your depth of feelings show.

In the aspect of abundance, a poverty consciousness will only serve to deny what you deserve. Abundance is good, (greed is not), whether it be material, esoteric, emotional or otherwise. Ask for what you want and deserve, and give yourself permission to receive it.

Self Definition

Being goddess is more than just alabaster skin and an Elle McPherson body. Apart from round abdomens and swinging breasts, common attributes of ancient goddesses include uncompromising strength, compassion and justice. Spend time working out who you are, who you want to be, and then honouring the true you in the image you present to everyone you meet. Do this by writing down the five most important elements that you want people to remember you by. Then live each and every one of these aspects.

Self Acceptance

If you don't love yourself, then don't expect others to. If you let others treat you badly, you are telling your inner psyche that you do not deserve better. The modern goddess gal never, *ever* allows herself to accept second best. Rally your personal power and self-respect and learn to say words like 'No' and 'Enough'. Most importantly, *mean* what you say! Also remember to give compliments freely. Affirm those around you, for if 'what goes around comes around' you will soon enjoy receiving plenty in return.

Self Expression

What you say is what you get. Expressions like, "I'll never be able to get over this obstacle," will manifest in exactly the way you describe. Instead of confronting and overcoming your fears, you will remain stagnant, bashing your head against the brick wall you say can't be knocked down. Change your speech habits to dispel negatives and embrace positives. Say "I can do it," and next thing you know, you'll be leaping brick walls in a single bound.

Self Reflection

Get over petty issues and open your vision to see the Big Picture. If you are absorbed in trivial worries, they are most likely a distraction mechanism to keep you from what it is you really need. If you had three months left to live, would you really care about your shade of lipstick or upgrading your mobile phone? Unclutter your life and feel how liberating it is to be in a state of 'simplicity'. Release those things that no longer serve you. It's up to you to prioritise what the important things really are.

Self Knowledge

See yourself as a minute organism in the ways of the world, both in the physical and non-physical planes, in the present and the future. Disconnecting with the world every now and then can be healthy if it lets you travel to a spaceless, timeless place of knowledge, wisdom, understanding and spiritual connection. To revitalise flagging energy levels, practice yoga and meditation when possible. Time poor? Take the phone off the hook and power-rest for five minutes – this time-out for self can be just as refreshing.

Colours For Chakra Animation

Colours resonate with your aura and persona to heighten, lower or balance mood. Surrounding yourself with appropriate colours thereby assists you to respond to situations with gracious power.

Base	Red
Sacral	Orange
Solar Plexus	Yellow
Heart	Green or Pink
Throat	Blue or Light Blue
Third Eye	Indigo
Crown	Magenta, Violet

Exercise: Colour the labyrinth

A labyrinth is a metaphor for your journey within. Unlike a maze, there are no hidden twists or turns in the path. Simply, a labyrinth is a winding trail that facilitates introspection for a deeper understanding of self.

You will find a finger labyrinth over the page. Trace the path slowly and deliberately with your non-dominant hand to become accustomed to the peace and quiet that such a simple task can induce. When you are ready, have seven coloured pencils on hand, and begin the following exercise:

Pause at the entrance and consider your current situation. Slowly and deliberately, colour the path red as you consider how this situation is affecting your balance and security. 'Walk' purposefully onwards with your orange pencil as you think about creative ways to resolve this issue.

Change to your yellow pencil to consider how or where you can source the personal power to deal with the situation.

Next, pick up your green (or pink) pencil and delight in the feeling of unconditional love that flows over you now. As you reach the centre of the labyrinth, know that you have the courage to overcome obstacles, and trust that you are not alone in your quest. Let love overflow through your pencil and onto the page; smile as you continue onwards.

Craft your words with your light blue pencil, and use indigo to finesse them with clarity. Finally, use your purple pencil when you can visualise the outcome of dealing with your situation.

Trace your path back to the beginning of the labyrinth as you reflect on this journey, and acknowledge the work you have done with the words, "and so mote it be."

Flowers For Chakra Joy

In imagery, the chakra centres are depicted as multi-petalled flowers. Plant life is representative of our own living forces – like flowers, our energies open to light and close to darkness.

Base

Red Clover purifies the blood, cleanses toxins and promotes a sense of purpose on your path; Honeysuckle helps you release the past; Holly reduces feelings of inadequacy, leading you to greater security and self-assurance.

Sacral

The little yellow flowers of the Evening Primrose relieve hormone-induced symptoms in PMT and menopause; vivid orange Poppies help you feel energised and motivated; the Pomegranate ('fruit of life') stirs creative energy and brings an abundance of resources.

Solar Plexus

Sunflowers represent youth, joy and resilient strength; Wild Rose restores your sense of intention; Dandelion improves appetite and digestion and lowers needs to over-achieve.

Heart

Pine relieves feelings of guilt; Willow brings about forgiveness of self and others; Carnation fosters healing, compassion, love, blessings and purity; Tulips celebrate love, harmony and beauty.

Throat

Kangaroo Paw facilitates words of kindness and sensitivity; Agrimony allows you to release fears and empower yourself through truth; Beech helps abolish judgement of self and others; Mimulus helps overcome shyness.

Third Eye   When at a crossroad, Wild Oat guides you
                 towards your innate spiritual gifts; vitamin-
                 rich Nasturtium improves sight on the
                 physical on intuitive planes; Geranium
                 protects against psychic attack or negative
                 energy.

Crown   Violets give you a sense of understanding of
                 the world, your life and you; Mustard clears
                 the weight of inexplicable depression; and
                 White Chestnut helps clear your mind of
                 clutter; Dahlia clears assumed emotional
                 baggage.

Exercise: Flow with the flower

Dr Edward Bach discovered 38 flower remedies to establish a
healing concept of 'flower essence therapy'. You can discover
the flowers that make your soul sing by listening to your
intuition.

Go out into your garden or a nearby park and take your
pendulum (or preferred divination tool) with you. Use your
intuition to guide you to flowers and plants that resonate
with each of your chakras.

Ask permission of each plant to gift you a flower. If you are
in a national park where it is illegal to pick flowers, sketch or
photograph them instead.

When you see your flowers, see your own inner beauty
matching theirs. Feel restored and free from self-imposed
limitations. Know that your flowers are here to stir your
creativity, inspire passion and promote visionary self-
expression. That they have come from the earth will help you
feel grounded and connected to your roots.

Gemstones For Chakra Power

Gemstones are gifts from nature herself. They resonate with different parts of our energy fields depending on their origin.

Base

Garnet balances libido, aids commitment and is useful in a crisis; Tourmaline grounds spiritual energy and brings protection; Bloodstone helps you accept change; Smoky Quartz allows passion to flow and fortifies resolve.

Sacral

Carnelian restores vitality and promotes trust in nature's cycles; Citrine opens intuition and promotes creativity and abundance; Brown Jasper is connected with the earth and detoxifies the body's organs.

Solar Plexus

Amber promotes drive to achieve goals; Tiger Eye brings integrity and empowers intention; Yellow Jade gently energises determination and helps eliminate waste.

Heart

Rose Quartz promotes unconditional love, inner healing and trust; Green Tourmaline brings patience, connection with others and compassion; Emerald is a symbol of patience and abiding joy; Malachite nurtures balance and trust.

Throat

Lapis Lazuli guards against psychic attack and encourages the use of the spoken word; Aquamarine promotes tolerance and releases you from fear of judgement; Turquoise enhances both earthly and spiritual communication for true soulful expression.

Third Eye	Moonstone facilitates deep appreciation for the cycle of change and lucid dreaming; Sodalite opens spiritual perception and is useful in meditation; Dark Aquamarine calms the mind and clarifies perception.
Crown	Amethyst enhances higher states of consciousness and repels negativity; Green Agate improves decision-making; Chalcedony promotes goodwill and telepathic abilities.

Exercise: Create your own gemstone grid

Source crystals that have a special meaning for you and your situation and place them strategically around your space. It could be around your body, or around a room. This is known as gridding.

You can create a chakra grid by placing one stone representing each chakra along your meridian – place them next to you in bed if you haven't got time to lie with the stones during the day.

To find more information about gemstones and their properties, sign up for the free e-Course *The 7-Day Chakra Workout* at ChakraGoddess.com.

Essences for Chakra Health

Essential oils generally come from plants and represent healing and living energy. The blends described herewith are based on the Goddess-ence 100% pure essential oil range.

Base Ginger is utilised to boost self-confidence. It is complemented with lavender, patchouli and palmarosa for their calming and balancing properties, and grapefruit white to energise and uplift your willpower.

Sacral Ylang ylang is used for its anti-depressant qualities to aide this chakra. To reach the centre of your creativity and personal power, sweet orange is used along with grapefruit white to relieve anxiety and patchouli for its calming effect.

Solar Plexus Lemongrass and eucalyptus are used to cleanse and decongest the chakra ready for the energies of rosewood, (used for its restorative qualities), peppermint to promote a pleasant sense of stimulation, bergamot to uplift, and lime and lemon myrtle to promote clarity and assertiveness.

Heart Sweet orange to reduce anxiety and clear the way for lemon (clarity), geranium bourbon and chamomile for balancing mood swings, grapefruit white to stimulate energy flows, and jasmine absolute – an aphrodisiac that brings optimism and balance.

Throat   Vetiver is used in this blend as a deeply
                  nourishing promoter of opportunities and
                  possibilities. Use with cedarwood to
                  decongest the chakra. This allows lemon and
                  cajeput to bring clarity and vision, lavender to
                  balance your new energy, and frankincense to
                  rejuvenate intentions.

Third Eye   Cedarwood atlas unblocks energy flows ready
                  for rosemary, a brain stimulant that promotes
                  clarity, calming lavender, frankincense and
                  lemon for rejuvenation, and basil to assist with
                  decision making in your new space of vision
                  and insight.

Crown   A euphoric state of enlightenment can be
                  achieved through the combination of
                  peppermint arvensis, clove leaf and cinnamon
                  bark, with sweet orange to keep you relaxed in
                  this heightened state.

Exercise: Blend your own essential oils

As these blends are being used extensively by
Aromatherapists, yoga teachers and natural healers, they are
suitable to have a go at blending yourself. Make sure you
only use pure oils (avoid fragrant oils as they are synthetic),
and be careful not to apply them directly to your skin if you
are pregnant or lactating – seek medical advice before
'playing' with pure essential oils.

You may read more about these blends and how to use them
at Goddess.com.au

Sounds For a Chakra Tune-Up

In quantum physics we can see that our bodies are made up of atoms and electrons that are in a constant state of oscillation. When they are hit by sound waves, they resonate with the energy of each tone or 'shape' of the sound.

Our voice connects our cognitive self to the physical world. Singing, chanting and toning are three ways to get energy flowing along the chakra meridian.

Likewise, sound waves coming *into* the body (not necessarily through your ears!) help massage your physical and auric bodies, giving you a sense of heightened joy and wellbeing.

Musical Notes

Base	C	*Throat*	G
Sacral	D	*Third Eye*	A
Solar Plexus	E	*Crown*	B
Heart	F		

Sacred Vowels

If you have ever heard groups such as the Gregorian monks chanting, chances are you have felt a sense of a cosmic connection while listening to their sacred sounds.

You can achieve the same state with these suggested sounds. Sing, chant or harmonise with them in repeated rounds. The power of these chants increases when sung in a group.

Base	LA	*Throat*	RE
Sacral	BA	*Third Eye*	AH
Solar Plexus	YM	*Crown*	OM
Heart	HA		

Elements For Chakra Direction

Incorporating elements into your life increases your connection with nature, both on the physical plane and in the greater world beyond.

Base	Earth	*Throat*	Sound
Sacral	Water	*Third Eye*	Light
Solar Plexus	Fire	*Crown*	Spirit
Heart	Air		

Exercise: Create a sacred space with elements

You may use a range of objects to symbolise each element and lay them out in such a way as to raise conscious connection with them. The layout below is loosely aligned with the directions on an eastern seaboard (with water in the east). If you live near a body of water to your west, rearrange this layout accordingly.

:: **Light** ::
lamp, candle, torch

:: **Air** ::
feather, fan,
balloons

:: **Water** ::
fish bowl, vase,
floating flowers

:: **Spirit** ::
journal, letters,
pen and paper

:: **Earth**::
soil, plants,
twigs, stones

:: **Fire** ::
candles, cauldron,
matches

:: **Sound** ::
CDs, musical
instrument, tuning fork

Symbols For a Chakra Shape-Up

There are many different ways to depict chakra energy in a visual format. Symbols that illustrate chakras can include multi-petalled flowers, Sanskrit shapes, or planetary profiles (to name just a few).

Here are some suggested shapes to represent each chakra.

Base	Square	*Throat*	Circle
Sacral	Pyramid	*Third Eye*	Star
Solar Plexus	Cross	*Crown*	Lotus
Heart	Chalice		

Exercise: Draw a mandala

Next time you're at the beach, close your eyes and allow your fingers to draw random patterns in the sand. If you can't get to a beach, use paint brushes on canvas, your toes on a frosty window or wherever your imagination takes you.

Focus on your ideal life as you let your drawing take shape. Do not look at your emerging mandala, but instead see yourself in your ideal life. What are you doing? What do you look like? What are you wearing, eating, hearing, seeing? Are you inside or outside? Who is enjoying this scene with you? What is it that you're saying to each other?

When you can see the scene very clearly, open your eyes and observe the mandala you have just made. How many chakra shapes can you identify? Ask yourself, do the most prolific shapes represent the energy that is driving you to achieve your dream, or is this the energy you need more of?

Alternative exercise: Create your own symbols for each chakra. Use the symbols I created in the image on page 10 as triggers to get your own ideas flowing.

Movement for Chakra Strength

Many yoga practitioners do specific exercises to stimulate their chakras. While there are dozens and dozens of poses that are suitable for raising vibration, seven poses in particular are recommended for each of the seven major chakras. These poses come from *The Goddess DIET, See a Goddess in the Mirror in 21 Days* by Anita Revel.

On a physical level, yoga is wonderful for promoting health because "… the asanas, or postures, lengthen your muscles, increase bone density, cultivate flexibility, encourage toxin elimination, promote blood flow and circulation, open the joints, release stale, stuck energy and emotions, and to cleanse and detoxify your organs," says Natalie Maisel, the creator of the seven yoga poses depicted herein.

If you're unfamiliar with yoga, please seek professional assistance to reap the benefits of proper practice.

Base: Warrior II

As you hold your posture, increase the effectiveness with this chant, "Conceive it, believe it, take aim to achieve it, let go to Athena, prepare to receive it"!

Sacral: Garland Pose (deep squat)

This is a variation of the Garland Pose, with the hands placed over the sacral chakra.

As you hold your posture, call on Aphrodite with this chant, "Aphrodite, Aphrodite, come to me, fill me with passion and creativity".

Solar Plexus: Utkatasana / Chair / Fierce Pose

Natalie also calls this the Nile Goddess posture.

As you assume this posture, draw in good energies of your choosing, and release that which no longer works. In honour of Isis, recite, "The Nile is rising, the Nile is falling, I bring in, and I let go," while maintaining the pose.

Heart Chakra: Seated Baby Cradle

Imagine you are
holding yourself as a
small child in your
own arms. Rock this
baby that is you. Feel
the love emanating
from your heart centre
as you breathe.

Chant a sweet lullaby
as you hold your pose.

"I am loved, I am
cradled, I am adored."

Throat Chakra: Butterfly / Baddha Konasana

In stimulating the
abdominal organs and
the lower body, this
pose helps shift
anything you're fed
up about. Release
pent-up, harsh or
unsaid words and
blocked feelings with
the chant, "Flow, flow,
flow."

An alternative for this
pose is to place your
hands over your throat chakra.

Third-Eye Chakra: Warrior III

Imagine you are
flying high above
pain, loss,
betrayal and
sadness. See with
your greater
vision and trust
your own process
in life's great
journey.

Chant, "I see, I see, the gift life is meant to be."

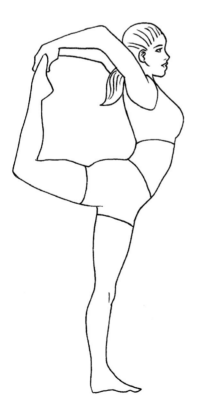

Crown Chakra: Baby Dancer

This pose fosters
concentration and balance. If
you experience difficulty
achieving it, listen to your
body for answers: what needs
to shift in order for new
inspiration to enter? Your
body already knows the
answer – all that is needed is
for you to still your mind, and
simply, listen, honour and
allow.

A suggested affirmation to
repeat while maintaining this
pose is, "I am eternal, I am
free, I'm filled with bliss and
harmony!"

Visualisations For Chakra Nourishment

By raising consciousness of each chakra via visualisation, you are empowering yourself with intention from within.

The following visualisation is based on the "Inner Goddess Tour" that features in a Goddess Playshop. (A Goddess Playshop is a fun workshop designed to heighten women's empowerment and well-being. At the time of publishing, this concept has expanded to include 60 Facilitators conducting these workshops around the world.)

First of all, sit in a comfortable position – it could be on your meditation mat, your couch, or even snuggled up in bed. Slow your breathing, expelling negative energy with out-breaths, and invite joy on inward breaths.

Walk now to a field of red poppies. See a pathway through the hundreds of rich, bold flowers and gently touch their petals and feel their energy as you stroll onwards. They make you feel strong and empowered, and you can feel their vibration bring you back to centre. You come to a clearing in the middle of the field. Take your shoes off and feel the rich, velvety earth beneath your feet. The heartbeat of Mother Gaia sends vibrations through your legs and into your belly. Va-voom. Va-voom. Va-voom… The Hindu goddess of destruction appears before you. Kali is here to help you purge elements of destruction in your life and reclaim your independent spirit by directing you onto a new path – your true path where you can discover prosperity, security and an easy connection with earth and humanity. You see Kali stomping her feet with all her might. Begin to stomp your feet in time with her, and continue your primal dance until you feel totally connected with earth and your true desires. Notice that the rhythm is beating out a message for you. What is the message?

Continue on, and find yourself in front of a huge orange tent. Enter the door and be amazed at the layers of the rich, orange fabrics lining the walls and ceiling – velvet, silk, and chiffon curtains billow all around you. The revitalising power of such abundance makes you want to drop everything – your cares, your worries, and any negative feelings and emotions – and to simply be playful for a while. You are happy to see Ishtar, the Babylonian goddess of love and sensuality, appear in the centre. She is spinning, dancing and shimmying to get your creativity super-charged. Invite her to guide your hips and belly in a dance of wild abandon. Laugh out loud as you spin, and notice your feet know exactly where to step and what to do. There is a mirror on one of the walls. Turn to face it, and admire the wondrous being you see in the reflection. That wondrous being is you! Ishtar is smiling over your shoulder and whispers a message in your ear. What is she saying?

Step outside the tent now, and see a beautiful maiden walking towards you. Meet Persephone, the goddess of Spring and Queen of the Underworld, here to facilitate your journey of self discovery at a sub-conscious level. She helps you take charge of your life, setting and keeping boundaries and believing in your amazing skills and abilities. Persephone invites you to follow her to a field of sunflowers with thousands of golden petals as far as the eye can see. She indicates your favourite easy-chair amongst the sunny flowers. As you sink into your chair and look up, the bright yellow petals create a vibrant awning over your head. Fluffy white clouds float past, the sun is warm on your skin, and you realise you are completely at ease with who you are as a person. You can hear Persephone laughing softly next to you. She tells you what it is that you have needed to hear for a very long time.

When you are ready, stand up from your chair and walk
onwards to a lush, green rain forest. As you enter the cool
haven, see a thousand different shades of green in the canopy
over your head; hear the calls of hundreds of her living
creatures; smell the rich earth, vibrant with life. A dragonfly
flits past and you are captivated by the green and pink hues
shimmering across its wings. Follow its journey with your
eyes and feel yourself uplifted by the feeling of unconditional
love flowing into every cell of your body. Breathe... Breathe...
Breathe deeply as Kwan Yin appears beside you, the Chinese
goddess of compassion, healing and balance. Feel her energy
embrace you – wrapped in her love everything is as it should
be; you are safe, you are valued, you are loved. It is easy to
feel gratitude, generosity and grace. And it is easy to trust,
forgive and to receive love. In this space, hear her message
help you transcend into a being of light, harmony and joy.

The path now reappears in front of you and you follow it out
of the rain forest. You step out into a lovely spring day, where
the sun is shining gently in a sky that is your favourite shade
of light blue. Here you meet Athena, the Greek goddess who
guarded the city of Athens and saved it from destruction. She
empowers you to explore your independent, clever and
resourceful side. She teaches you to let go of things that no
longer serve you. And she is the warrior woman within who
is freed when you speak your truth. Athena's sword is in the
ground next to you. It reminds you of a situation that needs
resolving with words. Maybe you have been biting your
tongue to keep the peace, or you've been nagging someone for
way too long. Pick up the sword and point it at the sky. Tip
your head back and feel the stretch through your throat and
neck. Relax your jaw muscles, open your mouth, and ask your
inner-Athena to yell or sing at the sky what needs to be said.

Place Athena's sword back in the ground and continue along the path. Notice how clearly you can see it even though the day is ending and the sky is now a deeper shade of blue. Your vision and clarity is thanks to Isis, the Egyptian High Priestess and her gifts of divine insight and trust. She is opening your psychic faculties and your ability to see on the non-physical planes. She is leading you to the shore of a large lake with still blue water reaching to the horizon. You can see feathery clouds reflected on the surface and smooth river rocks resting on the bottom of the shallows. Look into the depths of the lake and allow yourself to be mesmerised by the reflections playing on the surface. Gently, ask yourself a question. What is the answer that you see in the water, either reflected on the mirror-like surface or appearing beneath? Trust... Trust... Trust that the answer presenting itself to you is correct.

Night is approaching as you leave the lake. Dusk becomes a warm, balmy evening but you can still see your way clearly on the path. Look up and see a million stars sparkling in the deep purple sky. How wonderful to be even the tiniest part of this magnificent Universe. Feel a sense bliss as you reach for the stars and feel yourself being lifted by Nuit, the Egyptian goddess who is the bridge between heaven and earth. She fosters within you faith, wisdom and a beautiful connection with your higher consciousness. You understand what it is to trust, to know, and to accept that you are love. Feel weightless and free as you are carried safely over the earth and sent soaring through the heavens. Trust... Trust... Trust, and allow yourself to fall into Nuit's loving embrace for a connection to her gift of bliss. She is now taking you to her greater world beyond – that timeless, spaceless place of all-knowing. Be amazed as you enter this realm, and know that, YES, miracles happen. What is the miracle being granted to you now?

When you are ready, come back to earth and back into your body. Make notes of the messages you received. Over the next few hours, focus on these messages and turn them into affirmations.

Keep repeating your new affirmations until they become habit and a part of your DNA. Over time, repeated habits become your manifested reality.

Notes on messages received

Date: _____ Mood: _____

Messages: _____

_____

Affirmation: _____

Date: _____ Mood: _____

Messages: _____

_____

Affirmation: _____

Date: _____ Mood: _____

Messages: _____

_____

Affirmation: _____

Affirmations For Chakra Grounding

An affirmation is a short, positive statement that describes an ideal outcome of a wish or desire. By identifying what you want from your life and expressing it in words as though it has already come to fruition, you are sending a clear message to the Universe of what you want it to provide.

The affirmation you choose must be a dedicated belief, not just an ad hoc approach to 'trying it out'. Be prepared to free yourself from insecurities and judgements that limit your potential. Using affirmations with your full commitment replaces negative elements with unlimited potential.

Choose an affirmation and work with it dozens of times daily, seven days a week, every day until your affirmation manifests as your reality.

Believe without fear or guilt that your desire will come true. Know that you truly deserve what you are asking for.

There are many variations and outcomes possible. They can be spoken out aloud, recorded in your private diary repetitively, or written on individual sticky notes and hung around your daily environment. Do what works for you.

Base	My path reveals itself to me
	I am exactly where I need to be
	I have the energy to do all I want to do
Sacral	I am woman – sexy and wise
	My creativity flows easily
	I have wonderful gifts and abilities
Solar Plexus	I am protected and loved
	I deserve to be treated with respect
	I am valuable, self-confident and strong

Heart	I live in perfect love and trust
	Self-acceptance brings me joy
	My heart is open to loving relationships
Throat	I am safe to speak my truth
	I invite new choices into my life
	I release the past and welcome my future
Third Eye	I trust my intuition
	I see the goddess' gifts all around me
	Every choice I make is the right one
Crown	I choose joy
	Connection to bliss is easy
	I am a child of the Universe
	I have all the time in the world

Exercise: Write your own affirmation

Imagine that a genie popped out of a bottle and granted you a wish. Perhaps you asked to lose weight. Focus on how you feel after the magic wand has been waved and the wish fulfilled. Are you now comfortable in your body and clothes? Are you feeling fitter? Stronger? More alive? If so, your affirmation could be, "I am a happy, healthy and fit size 12."

Your affirmation should always be written in present tense. Using words like 'will do' keeps your outcome in the future out of your reach. It should also be written using positive words – the Universe does not acknowledge words such as 'not'. For example, if you say "I am not poor" the Universe hears "I am poor". Ask instead for, "I have enough money for all that I need."

Have some fun and try the specially designed affirmation booster at www.goddess.com.au/affirmations_booster.htm

Goddess Messages For Empowerment

Modern women have many faces. In just one day, you can be Ms Professional at work; partner, cook and carer at home; and Social Queen with friends. Using the ancient goddesses as role models is one way to get through each day with your integrity intact.

Herewith, 49 goddesses offer messages that you can use as a mantra in the face of any situation. Each mantra raises conscious energy, thereby empowering you from within.

Base	Freja	Feel Passion
	Kali	Embrace Change
	Cordelia	Stand Firm
	Gaia	Exist in Peace
	Lilith	Strive for Balance
	Artemis	Stay Strong
	Venus	Enjoy Decadence
Sacral	Baubo	Laugh Out Loud
	Ceres	Nourish Body+Soul
	Aphrodite	Emit Magnetism
	Eostre	Seek Fresh Starts
	Demeter	Stay Determined
	Ishtar	Discover the Divine
	Tyche	Create Luck
Solar Plexus	Astarte	Be Resilient
	Pele	Inspire Vitality
	Oya	Simplify Matters
	Persephone	Prove Personal Power
	Diana	Pursue Adventure
	Bodicea	Focus Your Energy
	Maia	Explore Options

Heart	Kwan Yin	Embody Love
	Amaterasu	Radiate Light
	Hina	Promote Growth
	Tara	Practise Compassion
	Hestia	Learn to 'Be
	Vesta	Nurture Self
	Juno	Connect With Others
Throat	Fortuna	Find Fortune
	Rhiannon	Use Your Voice
	Dana	Share Your Story
	Sri Laxmi	Deserve Abundance
	Athena	Speak Your Truth
	Iambe	Play With Words
	Oshun	Go With the Flow
Third Eye	Hathor	Reinvent Yourself
	Baba Yaga	Have Faith
	Isis	Trust Your Choices
	Cerridwen	Manifest Magic
	Brigid	See Your Path
	Inanna	Be Perfectly Honest
	Epona	Live Your Dream
Crown	Spider Woman	Believe in Dreams
	Circe	See Choices
	Hecate	Follow Your Intuition
	IxChel	Revel in Womanhood
	Yemaya	Find Comfort
	Bast	Relish Joy
	Nuit	Experience Bliss

Which Goddess Energy is With You Now?

Take a minute to complete this simple exercise to determine which ancient goddess energy is inspiring you today. By being conscious of that energy, you will be able to harness it more effectively in order to attain your highest ideals when dealing with those around you.

Remove yourself from distractions while you look at each of the pictures below. Take all the time you need to work out which particular shape 'speaks' to you the loudest. Find that image on the following page to read about which goddess energy is working with you at this moment.

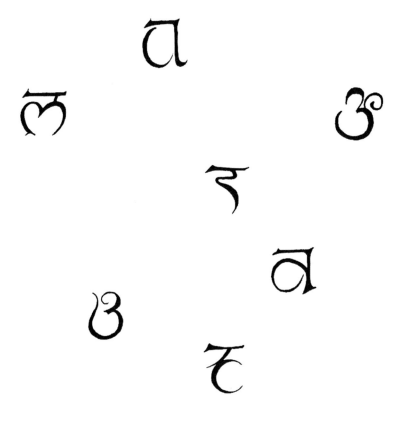

Ready Reckoner: Which Symbol?

Find the symbol you resonated with the most and turn to the relevant page for the next step in this intuitive exercise.

 BASE CHAKRA :: Go to page 47

 SACRAL CHAKRA :: Go to page 53

 SOLAR PLEXUS CHAKRA :: Go to page 59

 HEART CHAKRA :: Go to page 65

 THROAT CHAKRA :: Go to page 71

 THIRD EYE CHAKRA :: Go to page 77

 CROWN CHAKRA :: Go to page 83

Base

If you chose this image, your self-confidence may be under threat, or you may be at a crossroads in life. Power up your base chakra to revive willpower and your sense of intention.

Choose a number between one and seven. Find the goddess corresponding to your number in the following pages to energise your survival instincts.

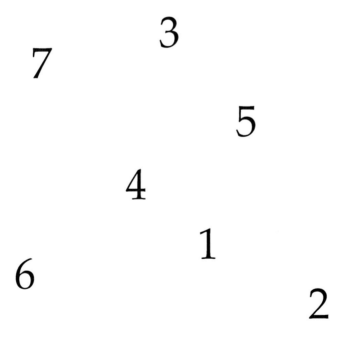

1.   Freja :: Feel Passion

It is from this Nordic Goddess of love, war and fertility that
we derive the name 'Friday'. Patroness of war, she ends life
in order to perpetuate it – as fallen war heroes come to
understand as they arrive in her great hall in the afterlife.

Her modern energy: Freja loves all things that give pleasure.
She indulges in love, romance and lovemaking, and stops at
nothing to get what she wants (even on the war-path!) Freja's
gifts are those that make us overjoyed to be alive – passion
for tenderness, grace, compassion, delight and laughter.

Do this: If you are feeling stuck in a rut, list five things that
are irritating you, and five things you are grateful for. Burn
the list of irritations and focus on the good things that bring a
spring to your step. Friday is the day to get back to your
passion, and get your passion back.

2.   Kali :: Embrace Change

According to ancient Hindu tradition, Kali is the mother of
us all. She may be depicted as the ferocious harbinger of
destruction, but this is purely in order to facilitate change.

Her modern energy: Kali loves your excellent judgement,
strong willpower and penetrative insight, but if you won't
do anything to get yourself out of a negative situation, watch
out. These skills are no match for Kali when she decides it is
time to turn your life upside down. This is simply her way
guiding you to a new path that will ultimately prove to be
more fulfilling than your current path.

Do this: Carry a red stone (such as a garnet) or wear red
underwear to give you the strength to confront the forces
that threaten you and to purge the elements of destruction in
your life.

3.   Cordelia :: Stand Firm

Welsh goddess of summer flowers, Cordelia is honoured as the Queen of May and of the fairies. She was the target of ardent attention from suitors competing to win her love.

Her modern energy: Cordelia defied her sea-god father's wishes and married the man of her choice. In doing so, she sent a very clear message that despite her flowery and joyful energies, it is good to stand firm so good things can come your way.

Do this: You don't need to go so far as to marry someone to emulate Cordelia, but you can become the heroine of your own story and stand your ground in the face of fear, threats or adversity. Place red flowers on your desk or home to keep her floral energy at a conscious level.

4.   Gaia :: Exist in Peace

The Romans believed every element in the Universe, on land, in the sea or sky, was a single living entity of Gaia, the primordial Great Mother.

Her modern energy: Gaia connects us to the universal source of 'earth mothering', leading us to a sense of profound peace and balance. Fortunately, her mother love requires no faith – simply appreciate her manifestation in everything you see around you. She is the living, conscious planet who provides sustenance to all life, whether it's to the smallest sparrow, whitest rose, stars in the sky, or *you*.

Do this: Tune into every wavelength of the millions of life forces around you right now. Feel the breeze on your cheeks and the rocks beneath your feet; hug a tree and lie in the grass; count ants and marvel at elephants – these are all Gaia's gifts to you.

5.   Lilith :: Strive For Balance

The first feminist and liberationist, this Sumerian and Hebrew goddess was honoured for her wisdom, freedom, courage, playfulness, passion, pleasure and sexuality.

Her modern energy: Proudly holding the rod and ring representing Sumerian royal authority, Lilith strives to make modern life equal for all people. Her message is to stop judging your opposite sex and learn to respect them as your equal – Lilith wants you to nurture equality in your environment.

Do this: Internalise Lilith's bravery and strength of character and make amends with those you've wronged with prejudice or presupposition. Achieve liberation of your inner joy and passion by being completely honest and respectful of others.

6.   Artemis :: Be Resilient

Greek moon goddess Artemis protected the forest animals as fiercely as she protected her (and her followers') chastity. She was the patroness of life, ending it in order to bring about rebirth of 'good'.

Her modern energy: If you are feeling threatened by a project or circumstance that seems to be leading nowhere, don't be afraid to nip it in the bud, *now*. Artemis inspires you to rid your life of excess baggage. Keep your integrity by building a safe world for yourself. Know that you are strong enough to confront the forces that threaten you, and that you are entirely resilient in the face of destructive elements.

Do this: Attach a smoky quartz stone to your belt buckle or holster(!), and say **NO** to forces that inhibit or bind you. You are *indestructible!* You are *strong!* You are the mighty, resilient *Artemis*.

7.   Venus :: Enjoy Decadence

The Roman goddess born of heaven and sea was revered for her gifts of fertility, sensuality and above all, love.

Her modern energy: Venus-ruled women have a beautiful sense of style and enviable appreciation for acts of love, pleasure and romance. Venus encourages you to do what makes you feel like a woman, whether this be by emotional, physical or spiritual means. For example, it might mean taking a girlfriend for a Venus-inspired outing to a day spa, designer boutique, art gallery or the latest 'it' restaurant. Pamper yourself today to channel your inner-Venus. Eat lunch at an elegant café; smile and laugh often; wear clothes that make you feel feminine; and adorn your ears, fingers and toes with your favourite bling.

Do this: Paint your toenails red and wear your designer shoes. Everywhere you walk today, consciously radiate magnetism and inspire others with your warm persona.

What Would Venus Do?

... she would draw on her innate sense of style and first-class appreciation for acts of love, pleasure and romance. She would do what makes her feel womanly. And, she would radiate a warm, magnetic aura.

Excerpt from *What Would Goddess Do? A Journal For Channelling Divine Guidance* by Anita Revel.

Notes about my base chakra

Date: _____ Goddess: _____

Observations: _____

_____

_____

Date: _____ Goddess: _____

Observations: _____

_____

_____

Date: _____ Goddess: _____

Observations: _____

_____

_____

Date: _____ Goddess: _____

Observations: _____

_____

_____

Sacral

If you are lacking in creativity, self-gratification, abundance or sexuality, call on a sacral chakra goddess to energise your fluidity and grace.

Which of the numbers below speaks to you the most? Find the goddess corresponding to your number in the following pages to energise your femininity and invite a run of good luck, creativity and abundance.

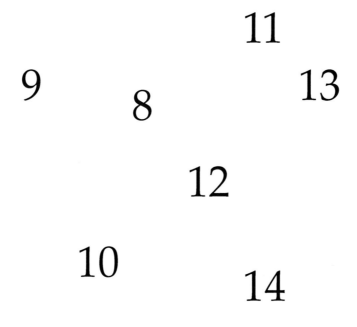

8.   Baubo :: Laugh Out Loud

Baubo, the ancient Grecian goddess, is a wild goddess of sacred sexuality. Her cheeky antics brought the grieving Demeter out of her misery, saving the world from famine.

Her modern energy: Mirth, sexual liberty and carefree joy are Baubo's themes. She thrives on merriment to restore female balance, beauty and strength. Watch your step – you never know when she might lift her skirts and catch you off-guard with a mischievous trick and a raucous giggle. When she does, take it as a timely reminder to relish sex, love and laughter.

Do this: Wear orange clothing to stimulate your sacral chakra. Stand outdoors, place your palms beneath your navel and breathe deeply into your belly. Laugh out loud with all your energy. Invite your neighbours to join in too!

9.   Ceres :: Nourish Body and Soul

Earth Mother, Ceres, is the Roman goddess of agriculture and the wheel of the year.

Her modern energy: Ceres represents the seasonal and monthly cycles we experience as women. She allows us to accept the ebbs and flows of nature graciously. If you are feeling that your energy is ebbing somewhat, don't worry – your body is simply slowing down to nurture your inner self to help cope with the pull of the moon and planets. Take time out and look after yourself for once.

Do this: 'Go with the flow' and indulge in what you want to do today. Eat a hearty meal with lots of vegetables and crusty bread. Make the effort to really taste your food. Chew it slowly, deliberately and with loads of gratitude. Notice how much more satisfied you are after the meal.

10.   Aphrodite :: Emit Magnetism

According to myth, Aphrodite emerged as a nymph from the waves and drove almost every male god wild with desire. Thus she is known as the goddess of love and beauty.

Her modern energy: Do you wish you could drive lovers wild too? Well, the good news is, you can. The aura you exude is the aura you attract. This means you can be a magnet for love by exuding self-love, but first you have to stop those annoying self-criticisms. Regardless of your shape or size, love your womanly attributes and allow your magnetic charisma to shine through.

Do this: Carry Citrine to manifest an abundance of party invitations: swing those hips, flirt and *smile* and you'll soon be celebrated as the life of the party!

11.   Eostre :: Seek Fresh Starts

Eostre was the Anglo-Saxon goddess of the dawn, from whom 'East' (where the sun rises) and 'Easter' got their names. When she tired of her lover, Lepus the rabbit, she flung him into the heavens where he remains to this day as 'Eostre's Bunny' (beneath Orion's feet in the night sky).

Her modern energy: Eostre is the goddess of fertility, spring and new beginnings. Take this opportunity to embrace her passion for new life. Now is the time to steer your own life in the new direction you have wanted for so long. Plant the seeds of new ideas, new jobs or new goals.

Do this: Do this symbolically with seedlings in a garden or window box. By spring, when your 'new idea' manifests itself in the form of luscious flowers, celebrate by frolicking in your garden, (sky-clad if you dare!)

12.   Demeter :: Stay Determined

In Greek mythology, Demeter is the goddess of the harvest. She represents the matron aspect of the triple goddess, and her daughter, Persephone, the maiden. (Hecate completes the maiden-matron-maven trinity, for your reference.)

Her modern energy: When Persephone was abducted to the underworld, Demeter's search took her on the path of poverty, abuse and eventually madness. If you continue to let a particular project or cause get the better of you this may be your experience too. Be careful you don't smother (as opposed to 'mother') the project you feel responsible for. With patient and gentle perseverance your determination will pay off in the end, as devoted motherhood always does.

Do this: Rose quartz will help you stay compassionate while succeeding in your quest. Place three pieces of carnelian next to the phone to help it ring with offers of help. Delegate tasks in order to reduce your stress load.

What Would Demeter Do?

If Demeter were in your situation, she'd pull out all stops to mother a cause. She would up the ante on the safety of her children or pet projects, and she she would lavish her mother love on all her loved ones.

Excerpt from *What Would Goddess Do? A Journal For Channelling Divine Guidance* by Anita Revel.

13.   Ishtar :: Discover the Divine

Descended from love-goddess Venus, is it any wonder Babylonian goddess Ishtar represents the fullness of womanhood and dares us to dream?

Her modern energy: Ishtar's energy represents love, fertility, passion and sexuality. Call on her when you need an energy boost to empower you as 'woman', and to achieve balance as a nurturing mother, inspired companion, playful bed partner, wise advisor, insightful leader or wild woman... Ishtar's energy resides within – all you need to do is ask.

Do this: Full moon energy is perfect for joyful acts of love-making. If you currently have no lover, join a drumming group with other women and play tribal rhythms under the moon. Also wear clothes or jewellery that contain Ishtar's symbolism – stars, the moon, the lion or the dove.

14.   Tyche :: Create Luck

Tyche (pronounced Tee-chee) is the Greek goddess of fortune. She was actually rather fickle with her responsibilities, entrusting the nitty-gritty to her assistant while she ran about juggling a ball.

Her modern energy: Tyche bestows protection, prosperity, success and good luck. Or not, depending on her mood. So if you feel that luck is passing you by, or you are a victim to the vagaries of fate, this is Tyche's influence. She is proving the capriciousness of life and luck and the erratic manner in which she decides the fortunes of mortals. The only way you can influence Tyche's dice to roll in your favour is to help others improve their fortune. Offer your resources willingly, whether it be financial, time or expertise, to help others grow.

Do this: Find someone who needs help, and give it willingly. Carry dice to keep Tyche's energy at a conscious level.

Notes about my sacral chakra

Date: _____ Goddess: _____

Observations: _____

_____

_____

Date: _____ Goddess: _____

Observations: _____

_____

_____

Date: _____ Goddess: _____

Observations: _____

_____

_____

Date: _____ Goddess: _____

Observations: _____

_____

_____

Solar Plexus

Personal power is housed in our solar plexus chakra, allowing us to be energetic, efficient and spontaneous through charismatic and truthful authority.

Which of the numbers below speaks to you the most? Find the goddess corresponding to your number in the following pages to recharge and revitalise your personal power.

18

17

16   21

19

15

20

15.   Astarte :: Be Resilient

Warrior Queen Astarte is the strong and wise queen of
Heaven. She was also the Greek goddess of love and fertility,
fire and productivity, war and victory and sexual prowess.

Her modern energy: Astarte-inspired women have an
uncanny knack to make the most of a limited amount of
resources with creativity and self-confidence. Be careful you
don't raise Astarte's sword too high in your quest though –
hostility only leads to self-destruction. Examine cleverer
ways you can achieve 'victory' with patience, respect and
wisdom and all these attributes will come back to you in the
way other people treat you.

Do this: Carry a tiger eye gemstone for energy and a white
stone to keep your intentions pure. Make 'Be Resilient' your
mantra until the situation has been resolved.

16.   Pele :: Inspire Vitality

Pele is the Hawaiian goddess whose spirit dwells inside the
largest active volcano in Hawaii.

Her modern energy: Pele-empowered gals are full of
passionate energy but can succumb to anxiety if the energy
isn't expended wisely. If you feel 'butterflies' in your solar
plexus, Pele's vibrations are confirming what you already
know on a subconscious level – your energy is being
misdirected and you need to do something about it. Come
out of denial, cut your losses and work to channel your
energy in a more rewarding way.

Do this: Carry a piece of lava rock while you conceptualise
what you want to happen. Repeat your vision often, both on
paper and out aloud. A positive thought repeated becomes a
positive habit which in turn becomes manifested reality.

17.   Oya :: Simplify Matters

Oya is an African goddess of storms, tempests and rain. She wreaks destruction in order to prepare for underlying calm.

Her modern energy: If you are chasing a leadership role, you'll learn it's not always an easy quest. Oya gives you the strength you need, but be aware of consequences – the winds of change may not be selective about what gets blown away! Look out, she says… your passion buried in the feminine psyche is being unleashed. Brace yourself to be tossed in her storms but be comforted in the knowledge that she is here to teach you about personal will and sense of purpose.

Do this: Release frustration and rediscover joy by jumping in puddles – without the rain we don't get rainbows (the symbol that represents the 'calm after the storm').

18.   Persephone :: Prove Personal Power

Persephone was the innocent maiden that was kidnapped to the underworld by Hades. But was it kidnap? Or did she go willingly in order to relish life on her own terms?

Her modern energy: It was only in visiting the underworld and coming face-to-face with the darker forces that Persephone discovered her true self. Everyone has a shadow-side – that secret place in the psyche hidden from public view. It's OK to visit this place occasionally, or to simply 'be' when this darkness imposes itself upon you. Allow it to pass, and it will. Accept your dark side as an integral part of your whole self to achieve unshakeable personal power.

Do this: Carry a yellow jade gemstone to keep you calm during your journey. Breathe deeply and consciously. Settle nerves and regain power by anointing your solar plexus with Goddess-ence *Persephone* blend of 100% pure essential oils. See you on the bright side!

19.   Diana :: Pursue Adventure

Diana is the Roman goddess of nature, fertility, children, providence and harvest. She is often depicted with her hunting dogs, deer and an archer's bow.

Her modern energy: Her short skirt is not for attracting male attention, but is a symbol of freedom – something every modern woman can use! If you're weary of your routine, the spirit of adventure-loving Diana is resounding with the wild places in your inner psyche. Don't let your busy lifestyle make time out seem like an impossible dream, says Diana.

Do this: Embark on your quest to satisfy the wild-child within. Get your motorbike license; run through a forest; frolic in ocean waves; hang-glide through a mountain range; go salsa dancing – do whatever makes your heart sing. It doesn't have to be complex or daring. Simply honour the calling of your wild woman within.

What Would Diana Do?

If Diana were in your situation, she would indulge the wild child within. Without hesitation nor fear of consequences, she would honour her need for adventure and escape to the outdoors.

Excerpt from *What Would Goddess Do? A Journal For Channelling Divine Guidance* by Anita Revel.

20. Bodicea :: Focus Your Energy

This great Celtic queen's name means 'victory'. Bodicea became synonymous with terror and savagery as she lead an army of Celts to avenge the rape of her two daughters.

Her modern energy: Like the tigress mother who protects her young, Bodicea gals harness their anger to seek justice on what they see as a wrong. If you want to scream, maim and kill someone who has hurt you, Bodicea's fierce anger gives you superhuman energy. Before using it though, think twice! In this day and age, not only is killing somebody highly illegal, it will also make a terrible mess on your carpet. Channel her energy so it is directed in the most useful area.

Do this: Light a yellow candle and visualise a better world for yourself. The best revenge is to live a wonderful life, so look deep within the flames to see how this can be done.

21. Maia :: Explore Options

Maia is the Greek goddess of spring, from whom we derive the name of the month of May.

Her modern energy: Maia is the shy and gentle goddess, patron of mothers and nurses, to whom sacrifices were made to ensure the growth of crops. Her traditional day of celebration is on 1 May, when to this day, men and women don vibrant green clothing and dance around a may-pole to welcome spring. Maia's spring-time energy gives us the chance to reflect on our achievements over the past year, and to examine where we'd like to go in the forthcoming year.

Do this: On the next clear night, take the time to star gaze. Maia is the brightest star in the Pleiades constellation, located between the hunter Orion and Taurus the Bull. Reflect on elements of your life that you think need Maia's influence of renewal. Use amber to fortify your intentions.

Notes about my solar plexus chakra

Date: _____ Goddess: _____

Observations: _____

_____

_____

Date: _____ Goddess: _____

Observations: _____

_____

_____

Date: _____ Goddess: _____

Observations: _____

_____

_____

Date: _____ Goddess: _____

Observations: _____

_____

_____

Heart

This shape is related to the heart chakra, the centre of empathetic abilities. Use goddesses of love if you have issues with self-acceptance that prevent you from connecting with others.

Which of the numbers below speaks to you the most? Find the goddess corresponding to your number in the following pages to find balance, joy and love in your life.

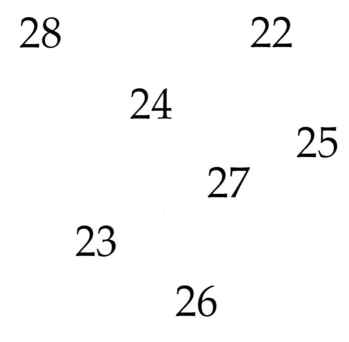

22.   Kwan Yin :: Embody Love

Kwan Yin is the Chinese goddess of love and compassion.

Her modern energy: If your mission is to make everyone happy, no doubt you are getting worn out and frustrated. Sharing the love is a good thing but keep it balanced between giving and receiving. The world needs Kwan Yin gals, but you are no good to anyone if you forget to look after yourself too. Your needs are as important as others' wants.

Do this: Carry a pink stone (such as rose quartz) and give yourself permission to take the world off your shoulders. Burn Goddess-ence *Kwan Yin* 100% pure essential oil blend to keep your home full of harmony and your life in balance.

23.   Amaterasu :: Radiate Light

In Japanese mythology, Amaterasu is the radiant sun goddess who ruled cultural unity, weaving and agriculture. Saddened by her brother's cruelty, she hid in a cave. She was lured out with laughter, returning light to the world.

Her modern energy: Amaterasu's flower is the chrysanthemum, a plant that flourishes if pinched back in spring, (whereby the growing shoots are slightly damaged in order to promote more vigorous growth). See the significance of this in terms of your own life – you too can grow stronger with each adversity you overcome. Amaterasu is a shining example of how your current situation can help you to 'blossom and bloom'.

Do this: Use the healing power of laughter and radiance to grow stronger. Place a mirror in an east-facing window to reflect Amaterasu's rising energy and dispel negative influences. Wear gold to brighten your persona, and smile to radiate the goddess within.

24.   Hina :: Promote Growth

Hina is a Butterfly Goddess of the Pacific Islanders. She is known as the first woman – hence the Hawaiian word for woman: 'wahine'. She lives in the moon, having travelled there on a rainbow path via the sun.

Her modern energy: Champion of words and ideas, Hina represents meaningful communication between women. She also facilitates the sharing of truth between the sexes. As a communicator, her inspiring speeches and ideas give birth to new ways of thinking. She is your inspiration to shine as a messenger, a carrier of news and creator of ideas.

Do this: Imagine you are a butterfly spreading her wings from the confinement of a cacoon. Draw on this new, delicious energy to create positive new speech habits. Banish negatives (such as *can't* and *won't*) from your expressions.

25.   Tara :: Practise Compassion

The goddess Tara has many different traditions. She is a Hindu symbol of eternal light and love, a Buddhist goddess of compassion teaching the wisdom of non-attachment, and a Tibetan goddess of love.

Her modern energy: Born from her mother's single tear-drop of compassion for humanity's suffering, Tara's energy is that of answering pleas for assistance. With her third eye, and eyes in each hand and foot, Tara sees beyond the mortal veil into eternity, gently reminding you that all things pass. "Each moment is perfect," she says. Be at peace.

Do this: Give an all-encompassing Tara hug to everyone you love today. Be open to receiving them in return. You never know… maybe you'll find it was you all along who needs the biggest dose of Tara love out of anyone!

26.   Hestia :: Learn to 'Be'

Greek goddess Hestia represents purity, sincerity, sanctity and safety. Hestia-inspired women love the uncomplicated, enriching and contented life she brings.

Her modern energy: In Greek art, Hestia was depicted in a pose of immobility. Similarly, you may be feeling stuck in a rut, unable to imagine living any other way. If the thought of a quiet, uncomplicated life is attractive to, take you a break from the situation that is devouring your every waking moment. Look for a life that let you to simply 'be'.

Do this: Now is the time to break your obsessive patterns. Establish new, healthy ones that nurture your mind, body and spirit. Repeat an affirmation focussing on mental, physical and emotional health.

27.   Vesta :: Nurture Self

Roman goddess Vesta was the Keeper of the Hearth and domestic life. In ancient times her temples were attended by her Vestal virgins.

Her modern energy: Call on Vesta when things at home aren't too great. Know that she is with you while look at your priorities. First things first, you need to take time to recharge *you* before you can throw energy into anything else. Eat right, stay active and enjoy the vices in moderation to help keep you healthy and vital. Use Vesta's enlightening and warming properties of fire to help you break free from the hustle and bustle of daily life for at least a short time.

Do this: Boil water on an open fire and enjoy a cup of chamomile tea while you block out the noise of modern life. Let yourself sink into a deep appreciation of all things natural and earthy. Your home will soon be a place of bountiful, healthy food and comfort again.

28. Juno :: Connect With Others

Prepared to go to any lengths to protect her relationship with her husband, Roman goddess Juno gives you energy to fight for the elements you want and deserve in a relationship.

Her modern energy: At some stage, everyone moves beyond the courting phase of love. If you are looking for a fuller commitment or a union with a soul mate, make sure you are truly ready to share your physical, emotional and spiritual self. Focus on elements of a relationship you hold most important: loyalty, fidelity, intimacy, inter-dependence, mutual respect, equality and so on. Be as willing to give these attributes as you are to receive them into your life.

Do this: Make a comprehensive list of the attributes that are important in a soul mate. Then reduce the list to five core attributes and repeat them like a mantra until Mr/s Right appears.

What Would Juno Do?

If she were in your situation she would be ready to share her physical, emotional and spiritual Self with her partner, on equally trusting terms as she receives him. Intimacy is not an issue when she is in a committed and trusting union. She would also foster elements of a relationship that bring it success: loyalty, fidelity, inter-dependence, mutual respect and equality.

Excerpt from *What Would Goddess Do? A Journal For Channelling Divine Guidance* by Anita Revel.

Notes about my heart chakra

Date: _____ Goddess: _____

Observations: _____

_____

_____

Date: _____ Goddess: _____

Observations: _____

_____

_____

Date: _____ Goddess: _____

Observations: _____

_____

_____

Date: _____ Goddess: _____

Observations: _____

_____

_____

Throat

This shape represents the throat chakra which is related to communication and creative eloquence. Tap into your inner goddess energy to 'find your voice' and overcome any self-expression obstacles.

Which of the numbers below speaks to you the most? Find the goddess corresponding to your number in the following pages to help you speak your truth.

34

31

32

35

30

29

33

29. Fortuna :: Find Fortune

Initially Roman goddess Fortuna was honoured as a fertility goddess. But she eventually came to symbolise abundance as the fickleness of life and luck followed the cyclic ups and downs of life.

Her modern energy: Fortuna bestows blessings only on those who deserve it. Her cornucopia overflows with items of goodness to sustain those who are genuinely selfless. To attract good luck and prosperity, ensure you are asking 'for the greatest good of all'. Abundance is not just about money and material goods, it is also about your spiritual, physical and mental self, and the needs of your neighbours.

Do this: Give something away – love, time, effort, praise. Set the Universe's circle of providence into motion; the more you affirm others the more abundant energy will come your way.

30. Rhiannon :: Use Your Voice

Wise and magical Welsh goddess of the moon, Rhiannon hears our wishes and guides us on the path of inspiration – but only if we learn how to ask!

Her modern energy: Keeping your voice locked inside doesn't help anyone, least of all yourself. Grinning and bearing a situation is *not* dignity and perseverance – it is just self-punishment. As Rhiannon grants the wishes of those who ask for what they want, and scorns those who do not, get busy articulating what it is you need to succeed in this project. Verbalise your wish or write it down to make it a tangible and authentic appeal for Rhiannon's help.

Do this: Repeat your wish over and over again as you plant a rosemary bush at the next full moon. Keep repeating your wish each time you use the rosemary in your cooking.

31. Dana :: Share Your Story

Dana is the mother goddess of the Irish fairy people, the Tuatha Dé Danann (*too-ha-day-dah-nan*.) They were skilled in art, poetry and magic, and ruled Ireland until they were overrun and driven to live in fairy mounds.

Her modern energy: Sadly there are no recorded stories of Dana – evidently her latent message is to tell your story before it is too late! So, stop behaving according to social expectations and simply honour your urges to be the heroine of your own life story.

Do this: Begin writing your life story... There is no doubt that you would have life lessons to share that perhaps you aren't consciously aware of. The words you write down today become an invaluable insight into *You* for future generations – what you stood for, the climate in which you lived your life, and the magical way in which you loved living each day.

32. Sri Laxmi :: Deserve Abundance

Sri Laxmi is the Indian goddess of prosperity. She is also known as the lotus goddess because she floats through creation upon a lotus – a symbol of purity and fertility.

Her modern energy: Though she is depicted with gold coins spilling from her hands, the creation of wealth is not her intention. Her gold, silver and precious jewels instead symbolises the awe-inspiring beauty of spiritual prosperity. In her aspect as goddess of abundance, she only helps those who are diligent and take pride in their work. Her message, therefore, is to act with intention and passion.

Do this: *Know* that you deserve abundance and that it will come. Ask for what it is you 'need', (this is different to 'want'), until your wish is fulfilled. Carry turquoise to enhance spiritual communication.

33. Athena :: Speak Your Truth

Athena was the beautiful warrior queen who stood guard over the ancient city of Athens and saved it from destruction.

Her modern energy: Athena-inspired gals are fearless, or that's the face they present to the world at least. They often put on a brave façade in order to keep their 'troops' motivated and united. You may be independent, clever and resourceful but know that people will think no less of you if you ask for help. Learn to accept help, and just as importantly, learn how to ask for it.

Do this: Wear a light blue stone such as aquamarine around your neck to help you release your fear of judgement. Dip the gemstone into Goddess-ence *Athena* 100% pure essential oil blend to support your efforts throughout the day.

34. Iambe :: Play With Words

In Greek stories, Iambe was a wild goddess of sacred sexuality who used poetry and witty comebacks to entertain others.

Her modern energy: Through creativity, humour and sexual liberty, playful Iambe is free to be true to her self. She relishes laughter and merriment to connect with her source of feminine energy. It's in the release of sadness or fear that female sexuality and joy is restored. Shakespeare recognised Iambe's creative genius and emulated her style – her iambic pentameter verse – in his plays. As both Shakespeare and Iambe knew well, it is easy to get swept away with such a seductive rhythm. It's no wonder it has survived to this day.

Do this: Rock in time to an iambic pentameter beat, feel the connection to the earth's rhythm as you rock to and fro, and become lighter and lighter in your outlook.

35.   Oshun :: Go With the Flow

Patroness of rivers and the bloodstream, this Nigerian goddess (also brought to Brazil and Cuba) was honoured as the goddess of love and sensuality.

Her modern energy: Oshun teaches us to 'go with the flow' of our instincts in order to find inner tranquillity. Just as water ebbs and flows, you can too. Be generous with your time for *you* during an energy 'ebb', and for *others* during a 'flow'. If you're overdoing it one way or the other, it won't be long before you're 'drowning' in frustration over the situation.

Do this: Sit on an orange blanket and gaze over a body of water. Let yourself wonder at its ever-changing face yet ever-constant properties. Give yourself permission to occasionally ebb away from the task at hand, knowing that you will flow back to them again with renewed energy.

What Would Oshun Do?

If she were in your situation she would go with the flow. She would relinquish control over her emotions and her expectations of others. She would dive into the Universal flow of life, fun and easy joy.

Excerpt from *What Would Goddess Do? A Journal For Channelling Divine Guidance* by Anita Revel.

Notes about my throat chakra

Date: _____ Goddess: _____

Observations: _____

_____

_____

Date: _____ Goddess: _____

Observations: _____

_____

_____

Date: _____ Goddess: _____

Observations: _____

_____

_____

Date: _____ Goddess: _____

Observations: _____

_____

_____

Third Eye

This shape symbolises the third eye chakra, related to the act of seeing both physically and intuitively. Use third-eye goddess energy to see clearly, in effect, letting you 'see the big picture'.

Which of the numbers below speaks to you the most? Find the goddess corresponding to your number in the following pages to help you clear your mind and focus on what really matters.

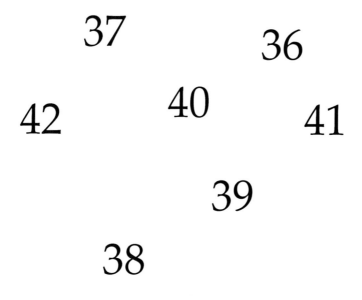

36.   Hathor :: Reinvent Yourself

Hathor was revered as the ancient Queen of Heaven, the patron of dancers, the mother of the gypsies and the generator of light and radiant power.

Her modern energy: Hathor gals have the gift of shape-shifting – the ability to transform yourself into whatever you need to be in order to succeed. Ask yourself, what is it that is causing you anxiety? Why are you allowing this influence into your life? What energy do I need to draw on to deal with it effectively? Take a step back from the situation and see the negativity for what it really is – a hindrance to the true 'you' showing her face to the world.

Do this: Visualise your favourite animal running free in its natural habitat. Feel a wondrous transformation empower you as you take in its energy throughout your day.

What Would Hathor Do?

If she were in your situation she would imagine herself to be the animal or personality that can easily transcend the obstacle.

Excerpt from *What Would Goddess Do? A Journal For Channelling Divine Guidance* by Anita Revel.

37. Baba Yaga :: Have Faith

The ancient Slavic goddess Baba Yaga is the wild old crone guardian of the Water of Life and Death, the mentor of old age, and of the life cycle of birth, death and rebirth.

Her modern energy: Baba Yaga says, you're not alone in feeling aimless and empty in spirit and emotion. But as long as you realise depression is not to be feared, you'll be alright. The process and emotion needs to be honoured before it can move on. Examine your dark side to empower yourself spiritually, psychologically, emotionally, and physically. Baba Yaga's job is to accompany you on your journey both there and back, so trust that she will do exactly that.

Do this: Wear black (breakdown of the personality), red (vital life force) and white (purification). Tie the scarves around a tree, say good-bye to destructive influences, and let the wind will carry your depression away.

38. Isis :: Trust Your Choices

Isis the Egyptian High Priestess, ruling with love and calm patience, who fosters inner wisdom and psychic power.

Her modern energy: Isis-gals are highly tuned into their own inner wisdom and self-confidence. Their minds are not cluttered with daily bunkum – rather, they are razor-sharp and able to make decisions with clarity and confidence. If someone is making you feel defensive or unsure about the path you are taking, choose to trust that your 'gut instinct' is your inner wisdom leading you in the right direction.

Do this: Use a pendulum or other divination tool to confirm what you already know. Ask 'yes' or 'no' questions and *trust* that the answers presenting themselves to you are correct.

39.   Cerridwen :: Manifest Magic

The shape-shifting Cerridwen was a Welsh goddess of enchantment, divination and dark prophetic powers.

Her modern energy: Cerridwen is the tigress mother who pursues her interpretation of justice with unfailing energy. She encourages you to go after your goals providing you're sure they're what you *really* want. If you have invested energy in starting a project, you have every right to see it to fruition. Shape-shift into a magical being in order to achieve your ambition. Choose a power animal to manifest their raw energies and bring their inspiration into your efforts.

Do this: Carry calcite to help connect your emotions with your intelligence and to allow Cerridwen's powers become apparent in you. Visit AnimalDreaming.com to research your power animals, and discover the wonderful work of shamanist, Scott Alexander King.

40.   Brigid :: See Your Path

The Celtic goddess Brigid is the benefactress of inner healing and vital energy. She is the traditional patroness of healing, poetry, and smith craft (her sisters carry the alchemical sword and blacksmithing tongs).

Her modern energy: All of these elements represent practical and inspired wisdom and creativity. Nurture your inner-Brigid during times when you have lost your passion, or for when you're feeling detached and you are drifting without goals and directions. She will help reignite your flame for living life with intention.

Do this: Write about your life in poetic prose. When you see your achievements written down for posterity you will feel more hopeful for the future. Then write a new chapter describing your ideal future life. Make this life happen.

41.   Inanna :: Be Perfectly Honest

Inanna is the Sumerian goddess of the dark moon, brave and unwavering as she ventures into the underworld.

Her modern energy: Stripped bare of possessions and dignity, Inanna almost died during a mission to the underworld. However, she emerged from her adversity revitalised and more powerful than ever. Heed the lessons presented to you in your journey. It is only at your most vulnerable that you will discover new life and increased powers. Don't be afraid to let go of old conditioning, release inhibitions, let alter-egos die and shed the burdens you carry.

Do this: Cry, sook, throw a temper tantrum! In dropping your brave façade, your true *You* will evolve into a stronger and wiser woman able to stay focussed and unwavering on your goal.

42.   Epona :: Live Your Dream

The maiden goddess Epona is portrayed as riding a white mare. As such she is the goddess of horses and travel. She fed her horses from her cornucopia filled with corn and apples, symbolic of mother-love and abundance.

Her modern energy: Epona and her white mare accompany the soul on its final journey to the other world. But during the day and in life she brings dreams to inspire you. Her message is that your future is full of possibilities, limitless choices and exciting paths to travel.

Do this: This week, allow yourself the time to dream. Give yourself the opportunity to let your ideas ride in your mind. Think of where you have been afraid to go and let the horses of Epona guide your spirit there in safety. Carry a ruby or moonstone for protection.

Notes about my third eye chakra

Date: _____ Goddess: _____

Observations: _____

_____

_____

Date: _____ Goddess: _____

Observations: _____

_____

_____

Date: _____ Goddess: _____

Observations: _____

_____

_____

Date: _____ Goddess: _____

Observations: _____

_____

_____

Crown

Self-knowledge and pure awareness is housed in the crown chakra. If you need access to deep understanding, wisdom and connection, use the energy gifted to you by these goddesses to help you rediscover your direction.

Which of the numbers below speaks to you the most? Find the goddess corresponding to your number in the following pages to help you connect with your higher consciousness.

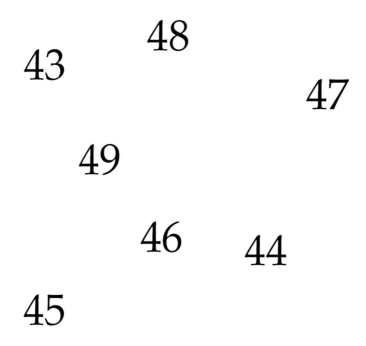

43. Spider Woman :: Believe in Dreams

Spider Woman, creator and weaver of life, is the great teacher, protector and Mother of all creation to many south-western Native American cultures.

Her modern energy: Have you been sleeping restlessly lately? If so, this is a sign that you are resisting Spider Woman imparting her sacred wisdom to you as you sleep. Open up to the possibilities presenting themselves to you through imagery. Keep your life-dream alive and continue weaving your vision, even in times of despair and unknowing. Spider Woman urges you to reconnect to our own spiritual source of higher power.

Do this: Purify your sacred space by smudging yourself with Sage and Cedar; sprinkle Goddess-ence *Nuit* blend onto your pillow before you go to sleep; enjoy astral travel on the threads of Spider Woman's spiritual filaments.

44. Circe :: See Choices

Goddess of the moon and the night, Circe began life as a 'mage for hire' in order to fund her expensive pursuit of magic. She was neither good nor evil, simply ruthless in her endeavours to further her own goals.

Her modern energy: Living alone on her island, the archetype of Circe is that of autonomous woman, self-empowered and whole unto herself. She does not need a man to complete her. Alone but not lonely, Circe's bouts of jealousy represents love in its irrational passion and remarkable power. This energy can be harnessed to enable you to take responsibility for your own actions and life.

Do this: Quit the mindset that 'life just happens' and apply your wonderful power to create your own destiny.

45.   Hecate :: Follow Your Intuition

Hecate is the crone witch goddess that shapes her subjects' lives in ways not obvious from a conscious perspective.

Her modern energy: Hecate's mysterious magic steers you in the right direction at times you feel at a crossroad. If you have a sense of foreboding about your near future, tap into your inner intuition (and Hecate's mysterious magic) to help you see the path ahead. Choose a divination tool you are comfortable with. Access the innate wisdom of your inner-Hecate to help divine your path.

Do this: Whatever you use to channel the divine power, whether it be crystals, cards, runes pendulums, tea leaves, psychometry (to name a few), have faith that the impressions presented to you are sourced directly from your intuition, and represent your choices.

46.   IxChel :: Revel in Womanhood

Mayan moon goddess IxChel is the mystery and joy of our female sexuality, mother of earth and all life, patroness of the healing arts, weaving, childbirth, and destiny.

Her modern energy: As fertility goddess, IxChel's power waxes and wanes with the phases of the moon, mirroring the fertility cycle in the bodies of women. IxChel says: Now is the time to celebrate life and love; renew and affirm your sensuality, kindle the fire of romance; make love by the light of a bonfire, the glow of red candles, or just the full moon's radiance; dance with bare feet connecting you to the earth.

Do this: Make a list of three things that you are going to create or manifest before the next full moon. Turn these intentions into affirmations and get serious about repeating them daily to make them happen.

47.   Yemaya :: Find Comfort

West African, Brazilian and Afro-Caribbean goddess Yemaya is Mother Water. She is the merciful goddess of creation and protector of women during conception and childbirth, and of children during their childhood.

Her modern energy: Yemaya asks you, whose problems are you trying to fix at the expense of your own well being? And why? Take a break from your struggle to surmount your problems or their source. Just for today simply accept the ebb and flow of the inevitability of the life cycle. Stop being the 'fixer', the 'nurturer', the 'servant'. The world will not end if you withdraw to take care of *you* for a while.

Do this: Carry ocean-sourced items (especially the conch shell), crystal and silver objects, and symbols to represent the moon and stars as you pamper yourself this week.

48.   Bast :: Relish Joy

Bast is an Egyptian goddess of the sun but was later adopted by the Greeks as a goddess of the moon. She was depicted with the head of a cat.

Her modern energy: As the ancestral mother of all cats, Bast is the patron of play. Bast-inspired women are energised with dancing and music, following a recipe for wholeness of body, mind and spirit. Quit subscribing to the patriarchal 'no pain, no gain' formula. Go with Bast on this – 'no pain, no pain'. You can have your cake and eat it too (what is the point of having cake otherwise?) Go on, indulge yourself. The simplest things can bring you the greatest pleasure.

Do this: Do something simply wonderful today. It can be childish or adult fun, but it shouldn't be difficult to organise. Do it again and again and make it a habit!

49. Nuit :: Experience Bliss

The Egyptian goddess Nuit is the bridge between heaven and earth. She represents oneness, bliss and universal love.

Her modern energy: Nuit-inspired gals have everything under control using calm love and understanding rather than fear or defence mechanisms. This makes them a first-choice source of assistance from colleagues and family, sometimes to the point where they are perceived as the 'all-round heroine'. If you are feeling overwhelmed from victims taking all your time and energy, tell them they can look after themselves from herein. You have more important things to worry about – like astral travel, moon walks and blissful meditation.

Do this: Carry an amethyst to help energise you with Nuit's cosmic energy during some Time Out. Take as long as you need in order to re-balance and find your centre again. Fall into Nuit's loving embrace with the Goddess-ence 100% pure essential oil blend named in her honour – sprinkle this around your meditation space to help you soar towards her realm in the stars.

What Would Bast Do?

If she were in your situation she would follow a recipe for wholeness of body, mind and spirit, finding the perfect balance between discipline and fun.

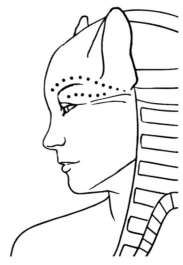

Excerpt from *What Would Goddess Do? A Journal For Channelling Divine Guidance* by Anita Revel.

Notes about my crown chakra

Date: _____ Goddess: _____

Observations: _____

_____

_____

Date: _____ Goddess: _____

Observations: _____

_____

_____

Date: _____ Goddess: _____

Observations: _____

_____

_____

Date: _____ Goddess: _____

Observations: _____

_____

_____

From the Author

Until I was well into my twenties, I didn't know I was worthy of wonderful things, doings and beings in my life.

Hard to believe huh? Maybe so, but it's true – this simple assumption that everyone deserves to live with respect, love and joy was foreign to me.

In fact, it was only since my first encounter with the goddess in 1997 that I realised a magical and enriched life was entirely possible... (Thank you Kwan Yin for visiting me in that fateful meditation!)

Having very little self-esteem at the time, I realised I had some serious work to do. Like finding and establishing a new set of morals and standards, for starters. Not an easy task considering my background – one where criticism and guilt had a firm hold in my DNA.

I wasn't ambitious for a miracle – I just wanted to learn my own worth and how to say words like, 'no' and 'help'.

It was a case of baby steps, baby steps to start with. But through dedicated and regular work incorporating chakra, intuitive and goddess wisdom I gained an insight into a life filled with meaning and purpose. *Yes!!!*

The first thing I noticed on this journey was that by my third chakra clearing session, the construction site in my head took a break. Demons such as Criticism and Fear had put down their tools. It was a remarkable feeling – one that I still remember to this day.

From there, Kali showed herself to me to help me under-stand my tumultuous life was her way of putting me onto the right path. I suddenly understood that I had to stop fighting blockages that were preventing me from going where I thought I wanted to go. For example, I was applying for jobs and being constantly rejected – Kali awakened me to the fact that deep down, I didn't want them anyway.

Once I embraced Kali's intention, everything started flowing. Great energy started to stream through me when I honoured intuition instead of waiting for 'luck' to happen to me.

I began authoring Goddess.com.au in 1999. At first it was a hobby – an outlet for the thealogical exploration. The process was both therapeutic and empowering.

In 2004 the Goddess-ence 100% pure oil blends came into my life. The blends were channelled then finessed with the help of an aromatherapist to create the product they are today. I feel so honoured to be the custodian of these amazing blends – every single week I receive emails and letters telling me how they were the catalyst that changed lives for the better.

By 2005, I decided that the research I'd been doing could be put to better use than gathering cyber-dust. So I overhauled the website filling it with resources to help others reconnect with their inner goddess. Dozens of new members join daily to receive a weekly inspirational goddess message… I am overjoyed to see so many women working to remember their true place in the world.

I endeavour to personally answer emails sent by members. If you feel so inclined, feel free to send me your thoughts, questions, comments and feedback via Goddess.com.au

Love and blissings,

Anita

About the Author

As described on Anita's personal website (AnitaRevel.com), Anita is a creatrix, author, mother and wife, web diva, dream weaver, lover of life. She's also a celebrant, teacher, artist, traveller and joy junkie but couldn't make these rhyme. Nevertheless, all these roles pretty well sum up her passion for inspired living.

Anita loves living with her family on a farm in the stunning Margaret River region of Western Australia. Her five favourite words make up the acronym BLISS: Beauty, Light, Inspiration, Sacred and Savvy. She has been known to interchange 'inspiration' with 'ice-cream' on the odd occasion.

The Chakra Goddess Oracle Online

 The Chakra Goddess Oracle is a free, online oracle based on the information in this book. It is optimised for viewing on your phone browser so you can access it anywhere, anytime.

The oracle uses the power of your intuition to reveal answers or insights that deep down, you knew all along.

It features messages from 49 ancient goddesses from various cultures, and presents their stories as lessons for the modern woman. The lessons are entwined with chakra energy to help you further understand the issues afoot.

Visit **chakra.goddess.com.au** to find which goddess message is waiting to reveal itself to you.

Other Creations by Anita Revel

The 7-Day Chakra Workout

Seven major chakras in the body; seven days in a week.
Coincidence? Or divine providence steering us towards
the perfect one-week chakra makeover? Anita Revel
developed this workout by adapting ancient theories and
applying them to modern practice. Focus on one chakra
per day for the ultimate personal and spiritual tune-up.

Selena's Crystal Balls (illustrated book for children)

Foster your child's emotional intelligence with this
illustrated journey through the colours of the rainbow.
The story encourages children to check in with the energy
of colours, and to establish associations between colours,
emotions, imagery and the seven essential aspects of life.

Sacred Vigilance, Wide Awake Meditation

Sacred Vigilance™ is an easy meditation style that
provides 100% of the benefits of meditating with 1% of
the effort. It doesn't involve quiet space, rhythmic
breathing, chanting, sub-consciousness, fasting, slowing,
or anywhere-in-betweening. It can be done anywhere, any
time – at the gym, at a café, in the supermarket queue.
And perhaps best of all, it's fun to do.

Goddess At Play, A Journal For Self-Discovery and Play

This journal is your receptacle for messages and insights you receive during a Goddess Playshop™. Reconnect your Self, intuition and Spirit, and see your Self as a perfect reflection of the ancient goddess archetypes.

The Goddess DIET
See a Goddess in the Mirror in 21 Days

Foodies rejoice! No more dangerous dieting; no more trash talking; no more self-loathing… When Anita Revel lost her libido, her self-respect and her aspiration to get another season out of her bikini, she embarked on a life-changing process to find her goddess within. In creating The Goddess DIET, she found dozens of Daily Intentional Empowerment Tools to realign her physical, emotional and spiritual behaviours for holistic well-being.

What Would Goddess Do?

This is a journal for channelling divine guidance. Restore balance and magic to your life by celebrating the highs and documenting the lows. Explore, create, play, ignite, animate and stimulate your divine spark with rampant gusto and grace. That's what goddess would do.

Lightning Source UK Ltd.
Milton Keynes UK
30 December 2009

148019UK00001B/234/P